ATLAS OF ADVENTURES

WIDE EYED EDITIONS

North America

Central America

South America

Africa

WORLD MAP

Europe

Asia

Middle East

Australasia & Oceania

Antarctica

N

W E

S

CONTENTS

THE WORLD IS FULL

Finland

England

Scotland

France

Spain

Italy

Germany

Russia

Alaska, USA

Canada

New York, USA

The Grand Canyon, USA

The Mississippi, USA

Mexico

Brazil

The Amazon

Argentina

Japan

China

Thailand

OF ADVENTURES...

This book celebrates the great diversity of our planet: with every turn of the page you'll come across different animals, peoples, and sights unique to each of the four corners of the globe.

Look out for our two adventurers in every scene as you travel through the book. What do they discover and who do they meet?

Follow their journey and be inspired to set out on your own adventures. The world is your oyster—what will you find today?

India

Israel

Morocco

The Zambezi

New Zealand

Korea

Egypt

Senegal

Australia

Hawaii, USA

The Antarctic

Iceland

Faroe Islands

Shetland Islands

Sail a VIKING SHIP (Norway)

Norway

Denmark

Go on a WHALE-WATCHING voyage (Iceland)

Blow the bagpipes at the HIGHLAND GAMES (Scotland)

Follow in the footsteps of giants at the GIANT'S CAUSEWAY (Ireland)

United Kingdom

North Sea

Ireland

See the sights from the LONDON EYE (England)

Netherlands

Belgium

Luxembourg

Go SKIING in the Bavarian Alps (Germany)

Atlantic Ocean

Go to SURF SCHOOL in Biarritz (France)

Look for treasure in Paris's pyramid, THE LOUVRE (France)

France

Switzerland

Liechtenstein

Explore a glacier ICE CAVE in Mont Blanc (France)

Monaco

Race a BLOKART in the Algarve (Portugal)

Portugal

Spain

Experience LA TOMATINA in Buñol (Spain)

Andorra

Mediterranean Sea

Corsica

Watch the HORSE-PARADE at Feria del Caballo (Spain)

Balearic Islands

Sardinia

EUROPE

Packed with dramatic landscapes, culture-rich cities, and wonderful wildlife, there is something for everybody to explore in Europe.

Go to sleep under the NORTHERN LIGHTS (Finland)

Take a SAUNA in Rajaportti (Finland)

Take a SNOWMOBILE SAFARI in Kizhi (Russia)

CANOE through the Dalsland Lakes (Sweden)

RIVER RAFT the Jägala River (Estonia)

Ride the TRANS-SIBERIAN RAILWAY (Russia)

Discover a masterpiece on the MOSCOW METRO (Russia)

BIRD WATCH in the Volga Delta (Russia)

Join a BALLOON FESTIVAL in Chelmno (Poland)

Go MOUNTAIN BIKING in the Carpathian Mountains (Ukraine)

HIKE in the Russian Caucasus Mountains and see Europe's highest peak, Mount Elbrus.

Visit DRACULA'S CASTLE in Bran (Romania)

Track BROWN BEARS in the Rhodope Mountains (Bulgaria)

Learn to steer a GONDOLA in Venice (Italy)

Save SEA TURTLES in the Peloponnese (Greece)

Visit the VOLCANO Mount Etna, in Sicily (Italy)

Seas
Barents Sea
White Sea
Baltic Sea
Black Sea

Countries/Regions
Finland, Sweden, Gotland, Estonia, Latvia, Lithuania, Kaliningrad Oblast, Belarus, Germany, Poland, Czech Republic, Austria, Slovakia, Slovenia, Hungary, Croatia, San Marino, Vatican City, Italy, Bosnia and Herzegovina, Serbia, Kosovo, Montenegro, Macedonia, Albania, Greece, Russia, Ukraine, Moldova, Romania, Bulgaria, Turkey, Sicily, Malta, Cyprus

BROWN BEARS are common in Lapland but hibernate in winter.

TAMASKAN DOGS come from Finland and can be trained to pull sleds.

The RED FOX has whiskers on its legs as well as its face to help it find its way through deep snow.

GO TO SLEEP UNDER THE
NORTHERN LIGHTS

SUNLIGHT HOURS are extremely short in winter in Lapland. In December, the sun barely rises above the horizon.

In the northern tip of Finnish Lapland, a small village called Kakslauttanen houses some of the most interesting places to sleep: igloos with glass roofs. These are built for the simple pleasure of viewing nature's most spectacular light show.

The natural phenomenon of the Northern Lights – also known as the aurora borealis – is the collision between gaseous particles in the Earth's atmosphere and charged particles released from the sun. The result is spectacular: a sky painted with bright green, violet, pink and blue brushstrokes, studded with stars and shooting rays. Marvel at the twinkling sky as you drift off to sleep, then wake up the next morning to a white wonderland where you can join a reindeer safari, ski cross-country or go ice fishing.

FINLAND

A WOLF'S howl can be heard over 80 miles away!

REINDEER have been herded for centuries by Laplanders for their milk, skins, and meat.

The igloos are made from THERMAL GLASS, which keeps you toasty warm inside!

The LIGHTS occur between 50 and 620 miles up in the sky!

SNOWY OWLS have a thick coat of feathers, which even covers their feet!

Lapland is said to be the home of SANTA CLAUS!

The colors of the AURORA are created by different gases: oxygen produces green and yellow light, nitrogen appears red, blue, or violet.

The NORTHERN LIGHTS are most visible from late August to April, when the nights are longer and darker.

RED SQUIRRELS are widespread in the forests of Lapland. They feed on the seeds inside pine cones.

CROSS-COUNTRY SKIING is very popular in Finland and was a useful way to get around many years ago.

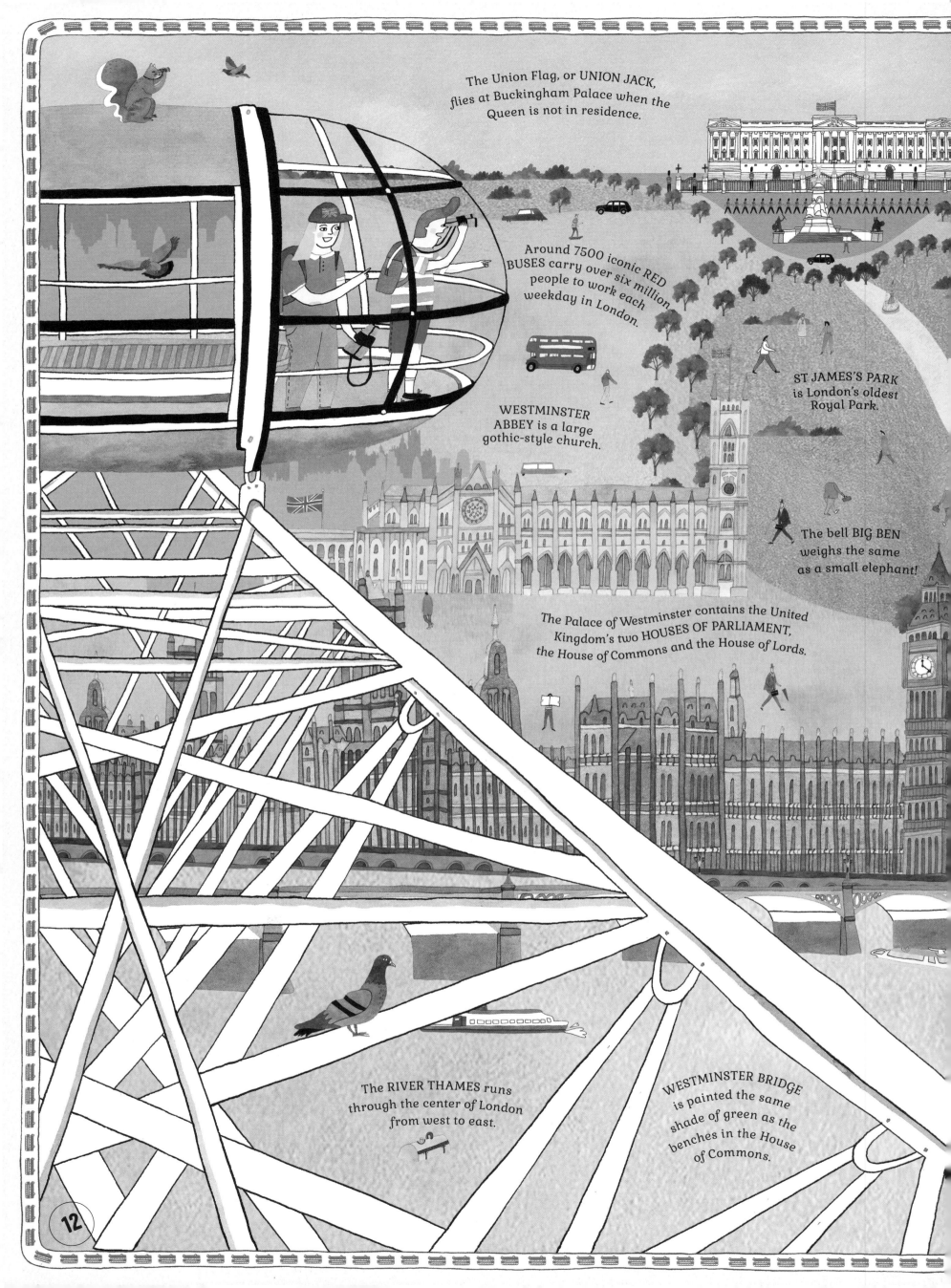

The Union Flag, or UNION JACK, flies at Buckingham Palace when the Queen is not in residence.

Around 7500 iconic RED BUSES carry over six million people to work each weekday in London.

ST JAMES'S PARK is London's oldest Royal Park.

WESTMINSTER ABBEY is a large gothic-style church.

The bell BIG BEN weighs the same as a small elephant!

The Palace of Westminster contains the United Kingdom's two HOUSES OF PARLIAMENT, the House of Commons and the House of Lords.

The RIVER THAMES runs through the center of London from west to east.

WESTMINSTER BRIDGE is painted the same shade of green as the benches in the House of Commons.

12

BUCKINGHAM PALACE has been the official residence of the British king or queen since 1837. It has 775 rooms!

GREEN PARK

The WOOD PIGEON is London's most common garden bird.

GREAT BRITAIN

THE MALL

BLACK CAB DRIVERS must pass the famous Knowledge test of 320 routes covering 25,000 streets.

10 Downing Street is the official residence of the BRITISH PRIME MINISTER.

The CABINET WAR ROOMS were located in the basement of the Treasury building during the war.

The THAMES PATH runs alongside the river. It is the longest riverside walk in Europe at 182 miles.

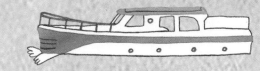

SEE THE SIGHTS FROM THE
LONDON EYE

Whilst London is England's capital city and has English as its national tongue, today more than 300 languages can be heard on its streets, giving it a distinctly international flavor.

One of the best views of London's teeming streets, historic buildings, and wide open parks can be seen from the western hemisphere's tallest observation wheel: the London Eye. Take your binoculars on a 30 minute ride in one of its rotating capsules, as 25 miles of the city's treasures stretch out before you in all directions. What can you see, and where will you adventure next?

Between games, the LOGS are soaked in water to stop them losing weight.

Competitors in the CABER TOSS are judged on how straight they can throw a large log of pine.

Pipers wear traditional HIGHLAND DRESS: a kilt, laced shoes, or ghillies, a pouch called a sporran, and a knife, or sgian dubh, tucked into their sock.

The BAGPIPES are Scotland's national instrument.

Scotsmen used to take their bagpipes into BATTLE, to intimidate their enemies.

To win the TUG O'WAR, one team must successfully pull until a mark on the rope crosses the central line.

BLOW THE BAGPIPES AT THE

HIGHLAND GAMES

Don your kilt, lace your ghillies, and pick up your bagpipes: it's time to go to the Highland Games! This celebration of Celtic culture and heritage began as early as the eleventh century. The biggest of these, the Cowal Highland Gathering in Dunoon, Scotland is held on the last weekend in August each year, and attracts more than 23,000 spectators and 3,500 competitors who participate in music, dance, and athletic events.

As "Scotland the Brave" fills the air with the massing of the bagpipes, you can witness the participants' strength and skill in diverse events which include the caber toss, the stone put, and the Scottish hammer throw. Look out for flying food: there's even a great haggis hurling event!

SCOTLAND

The winner of the STONE PUT is the participant who throws a heavy stone (taken from a local lake) the furthest.

It's thought the games began when Scottish King Malcolm III held a competition to find the best ROYAL MESSENGER.

People travel from all over the world to SPECTATE and COMPETE in the Scottish Highland Games.

Performers of the ancient SCOTTISH SWORD DANCE must dance between two crossed swords without touching them.

HAGGIS HURLING competitors try to throw a haggis as far as possible, landing it intact.

The Scottish Terrier, or SCOTTIE, is a breed of dog that dates back as far as the fifteenth century.

The FLAG OF SCOTLAND, also known as the St Andrew's Cross, is blue with a white cross.

HAGGIS is a traditional dish containing suet, oatmeal, and offal, stuffed into an animal's stomach.

15

The FRENCH FLAG, the TRICOLOR, has three vertical bands of blue, white, and red.

FRANCE

Paris is known as the CITY OF LIGHTS because of the number of artists, writers, and sculptors who made it their home.

LOOK FOR TREASURES IN PARIS'S PYRAMID,
THE LOUVRE

France's Louvre is the largest museum in the world and it houses thousands of art history's most treasured pieces. Egyptian antiques, ancient Greek and Roman sculptures, jewels, and paintings rest on walls and in cabinets of two different buildings: a magnificent, Renaissance and classical-style palace and a modern collection of glass pyramids, the largest of which is the entrance to the museum.

Here you will find world-renowned treasures like the Mona Lisa, the Venus de Milo, and the Winged Victory; but there are another 35,000 pieces to discover for yourself. It would take 100 days to see everything in the Louvre if you looked at each item for 30 seconds: so be prepared to put ample time aside if you want to see this challenge through!

The museum is situated on the banks of the RIVER SEINE.

The Louvre was originally built in the twelfth century as a FORTRESS.

The PYRAMID is the most recent addition to the Louvre and was opened in 1989...

King Francis I began the Louvre's collection in the SIXTEENTH CENTURY. Among other paintings, he bought the Mona Lisa.

It is made of GLASS AND METAL and designed by an American, I.M. PEI...

The paintings department at the Louvre now houses over 7,500 ARTWORKS!

This was the first ARCHITECT from outside of France to work on the Louvre.

The French proclaimed their love for POODLES in the 1500s when it was named France's national dog.

Nearly 10 MILLION PEOPLE visit the Louvre every year.

SPAIN

FLAMENCO GUITAR players rest on barrels of sherry in the square.

Spectators eat small plates of food known as TAPAS.

Each year the horses are decorated to match the fair's DIFFERENT THEME.

PAELLA is a traditional Spanish dish made with rice, vegetables, meat, or seafood.

WATCH THE HORSE PARADE AT
FERIA DEL CABALLO

"Ole!" shout the flamenco ladies to the guitarist as the first dance of the day begins at the Feria del Caballo, Spain's biggest horse festival. Here, it is not only people that dance: the colorful street parade is led by a group of horses who perform equestrian ballet!

The serious "horse ballet" competition begins in the evening, but when the sun is out these horses parade through the old town of Jerez de la Frontera, ridden by men in flat-topped hats, frilly white shirts, and leather chaps, and joined by women dressed in flamenco-style dresses. Learn your first steps with a flamenco troupe or relax by one of the many decorated tents, or casetas, with a plate full of Spanish tapas as the colorful parade unfolds before you.

Colorful tents called CASETAS are set up. Inside you will find traditional food, drink, and people dancing.

FLAMENCO DANCERS use expressive arm gestures and stamp their feet. Flamenco originated in this region.

Horsemen, or CABALLEROS, teach their horses to "dance"—prancing with their feet up high, jumping, and rearing onto their hind legs.

A brightly dressed woman sits behind the horseman in FLAMENCO DRESS.

The Feria del Caballo takes place every May and lasts for seven days, attracting over ONE MILLION VISITORS.

Flamenco guitar players, or TOCAORES, play complex melodies and knock their instrument rhythmically.

The ANDALUSIAN HORSE is famous for its elegance and strength.

Jerez de la Frontera is in a region of Spain called ANDALUCIA, which is known around the world for its horsemanship, sherry, and flamenco.

Feria del Caballo, also known as Feria de Jerez, has been celebrated since MEDIEVAL TIMES, when the town would gather to trade animals.

Venice is a city in northeastern Italy made up of 118 ISLANDS and connected by more than 150 CANALS and 400 BRIDGES.

In MEDIEVAL TIMES, Venice was one of the world's most important cities and attracted rich and powerful merchants to its shores.

Venice suffers from frequent FLOODING, especially in the winter months when the tides are high.

The first ever FEMALE GONDOLIER was appointed in 2010.

A GONDOLIER'S UNIFORM consists of a white sailor's shirt or striped T-shirt with a matching straw boater and a navy wool jacket in winter.

Gondolas are an ANCIENT FORM OF TRANSPORT and have been seen in Venice since 1094.

ITALY

Gondoliers must PASS AN EXAM before they are licensed to carry passengers.

More than 15 MILLION visitors come to Venice every year.

The entire city of Venice—known as the floating city—is gradually SINKING INTO THE SEA at a rate of 1–2 millimeters per year.

The RIALTO BRIDGE was completed in 1591 and is one of four bridges that crosses the Grand Canal.

Gondolas are ASYMMETRICAL to make them more manoeuvrable.

A law was passed in 1562 that all gondolas should be PAINTED BLACK to stop nobles competing for the most colorful and decadent boat.

The GRAND CANAL, or Canalazzo, is the largest waterway in Venice and divides the city in two.

LEARN TO STEER A GONDOLA IN
VENICE

The best way around Venice, Italy, is by gondola: so why not learn to steer one yourself? Gondolas are perfectly designed for negotiating the shallows and mudflats of Venice's canal system, and the art of steering one is centuries old. The trade began in medieval times and is practiced today in the age old tradition which has seen little change over the years.

Gondoliers stand at the back of the boat with their oar and propel the boat onwards with a forward stroke, followed by a backward stroke. Delight in a scene of beautiful palaces, fine cathedrals, and marble bridges, such as the Rialto Bridge, as you glide down the Grand Canal.

GERMANY

RED DEER look for food and shelter in the forests surrounding the Bavarian Alps.

Much wildlife hides in the thick FIR TREE forests.

Snowboarders either ride REGULAR, leading with their left foot, or GOOFY, leading with their right foot.

One young adventurer performs a trick called a GRAB!

When your legs get tired from skiing you can slide down the mountain on an INFLATABLE RUBBER RING!

FREESTYLE SKIING began in the 1930s. Skiers in Europe began adding flips, twists, and other acrobatic moves to their routines.

Ski runs made of compacted snow are known as PISTES and icy bumps are called MOGULS.

A small population of endangered ROCK PARTRIDGES can be found in this area.

SKI LIFTS

Enjoy a HOT CHOCOLATE... and a piece of BLACK FOREST GÂTEAU.

BLACK FOREST HORSES were bred to help with heavy forestry work.

Skiing is an ANCIENT SPORT— the first known pictures of people skiing were found in Norway, and date back to 4000 BC!

Skiers choose a ZIG-ZAG PATH down the piste, which stops them from going too fast.

Almost 24 MILLION PEOPLE visit Bavaria every year. Many of them come to enjoy winter sports!

Bavaria is one of the OLDEST STATES IN EUROPE, dating back as far as the sixth century.

GO SKIING IN THE
BAVARIAN ALPS

Like stepping into a scene of a Grimms' fairy tale, the wooded mountain range of the Bavarian Alps in southern Germany is a world of cuckoo clocks, cherry gateau, and wooden chalets. This winter wonderland is one of the biggest skiing destinations in Germany, and Sudelfeld is a favorite for downhill skiers of all kinds.

Find your fastest route down hundreds of feet of snow and ride the lift back to the top—and then do it all over again! This is a place where anything goes—downhill, freestyle, and snowboarding—there's "snow style" like your own!

Many people stumble across the magnificent AQUARELLE TRAIN by accident when they travel on the Sokolnicheskaya—or "Red"—Line.

The Aquarelle Train was launched on CHILDREN'S DAY in 2007 to remind commuters to look up from their papers and enjoy their surroundings more often!

There are three other special trains on the RED LINE: the Reading Train, the Poetry Train, and the Retro Train, which resembles the first train car to run on the Moscow Metro.

BAKED POTATOES are a popular kind of fast food in Moscow.

Although it is warmer underground, the people of Moscow aren't without a thick coat and hat in WINTER, when it reaches temperatures of −10°C outside.

There are 194 stations on the Moscow Metro, and more than NINE MILLION PEOPLE use it every weekday.

RUSSIA

The Aquarelle Train is named for its special cargo — the name translates into English as the WATERCOLOR TRAIN.

СЛАВЯНСКИЙ БУЛЬВАР

The subway is turned into a concert hall by skilled MUSICIANS BUSKING on the platform.

The ornate benches and lamps are designed in an ART NOUVEAU style. They were inspired by Paris's metro, in France.

The metro isn't only used by people; some clever DOGS have been seen taking the train!

DISCOVER A MASTERPIECE ON THE
MOSCOW METRO

You'd be right in thinking that much of the world's subway train stations are filled with old bits of chewing gum and day-old newspapers—but not in Moscow, Russia. The Moscow Metro began operating in 1935 with a single 7 mile line connecting just 13 stations, each filled with ornaments and artworks. Young adventurers will feel like royalty as they train hop from one station to another, marveling at the colorful mosaics, marbled walls, frescoed ceilings, chandeliers, and gold fixtures found in many of Moscow's underground trains.

Some lucky travelers may even spot the famous Aquarelle train pulling into the station, adorned in flowers like a moving painting. The Aquarelle runs an irregular schedule but is designed as a moveable art museum, with framed paintings on every carriage wall. Catching the train has never been so grand!

25

Beaufort
Sea

Greenland

SPOT A NARWHAL
in Baffin Bay
(North Atlantic Ocean)

Alaska (USA)

Davis Strait

DOG-SLED
with huskies in
Alaska (USA)

PAN FOR GOLD
in the Yukon River (USA)

Try ARCTIC CHAR FISHING
in Nunavut (Canada)

Gulf of
Alaska

SLEEP IN A TEEPEE
in Yellowknife (Canada)

Hudson
Bay

Lift off in a
HOT AIR BALLOON
in Quebec (Canada)

Discover ancient
TOTEM POLES
in the forests of
Haida Gwaii (Canada)

Canada

Send a puck flying
in a game of ICE HOCKEY
in Winnipeg (Canada)

Make MAPLE SYRUP
in Ontario (Canada)

RIDE A ROLLER COASTER
in Chicago (USA)

Be dwarfed by
GIANT REDWOOD TREES
in Sequoia National Park (USA)

Walk through a
GHOST TOWN in
Virginia City (USA)

CARVE A PUMPKIN
in Nebraska (USA)

United States
of America

Watch a ROCKET LAUNCH
at Cape Canaveral (USA)

RIVER-RAFT through
the Grand Canyon in
Arizona (USA)

DO THE HOEDOWN
in Texas (USA)

Dance on the
deck of a STEAMBOAT,
Louisiana (USA)

Pacific
Ocean

Gulf of
Mexico

Rattle your bones
at the DAY OF THE DEAD
in Mixquic (Mexico)

Mexico

Caribbean
Sea

Find a flutter of
MONARCH BUTTERFLIES
in Michoacán (Mexico)

NORTH AMERICA

Whether it's rock formations, roller coasters, or redwood trees, you'll be hard-pressed to find adventures any BIGGER than those that await you in North America! So go ahead and seek out your own American Dream.

Take a picture of a PUFFIN on the island of Newfoundland (Canada)

HIT A HOME RUN in Central Park, New York City (USA)

Azores

Atlantic Ocean

Bermuda

Sargasso Sea

DOG SLED WITH HUSKIES IN
ALASKA

See the wilds of Denali National Park in Alaska, America, from a sled pulled by an excitable team of dogs! Alaskan huskies are bred for strength and endurance and are trained to cover vast distances carrying heavy loads—including young adventurers.

Race by nature's most majestic beasts— including moose and caribou—then retire at dusk to a wood cabin for a dinner of fresh salmon by the fire. Just don't forget to feed the dogs before bed!

CROSS-COUNTRY SKIING is a quieter way to explore the national park in winter.

MOUNTAIN GOATS are found in the rocky, mountainous regions of Alaska.

The dogs wear PROTECTIVE BOOTIES made of polar fleece to keep their paws warm while sledding.

Alaskan huskies have a DOUBLE COAT with a thick, water-resistant undercoat and coarse outer coat.

At 20,321 feet above sea level, MOUNT MCKINLEY is the highest mountain peak in North America.

The North American BALD EAGLE isn't actually bald; bald used to mean "white headed."

ALASKA, USA

The DENALI CARIBOU HERD

DENALI HUSKIES help patrol the two-million acres of national park where vehicles are not allowed.

A LYNX is twice the size of a domestic cat and feeds on snowshoe hares.

DALL SHEEP can detect small objects from over half a mile away—without binoculars!

The ALASKAN MOOSE is the largest in the world: males weigh up to 1,700 pounds.

The ROCK PTARMIGAN has three seasonal plumages: it is brown in summer, grey in fall, and white in winter.

GRIZZLY BEARS love to eat salmon, which has a high fat content. This allows some Alaskan grizzlies to weigh more than 1,300 pounds.

LEMMINGS can travel far and wide in search of food, but seldom fish; they are herbivores!

LIFT OFF IN A
HOT AIR BALLOON

Wake up to a sky filled with... balloons! Long before there were toy balloons, hot air balloons lifted people in the air, and the first of these was designed by Etienne and Joseph Montgolfier in 1783. Today you can take part in a dawn flight at the international balloon festival of Saint-Jean-sur-Richelieu, one of the world's biggest hot air balloon gatherings.

The Canadian balloon festival began in 1984 and soon became a popular ballooning event, where professionals compete in races and visitors take scenic rides at dawn and dusk each day. A photo from your wicker basket, or "gondola," may be the most colorful picture you ever take, as more than 100 balloons of every shape, color, and size take to the skies.

A burner controlled by the pilot fills the balloon with HOT GAS, which is lighter than air and causes the balloon to rise.

The French MONTGOLFIER BROTHERS designed the first manned hot air balloon in 1783, but chose other people to fly in it!

The basket that carries you into the air is known as a GONDOLA.

A FERRIS WHEEL offers lifts to visitors not partaking in a hot air balloon flight.

There's fun to be had on the ground, too, at the world's LARGEST INFLATABLE THEME PARK, Balloon Planet.

The city of Saint-Jean-sur-Richelieu has a TRANSPORTATION HERITAGE, with important train and canal links to wider North America.

Unmanned hot air balloons called KONGMING LANTERNS were found in China as early as the third century.

CANADA

A MAPLE LEAF with eleven points appears on the Canadian flag.

Gondolas are often made of WOVEN WICKER, a material which is both light and strong.

In 1999, Bertrand Piccard and Brian Jones were the first people to fly a hot air balloon all the way AROUND THE WORLD.

Nearly HALF A MILLION VISITORS converge on this festival every year to see the colorful balloons take flight.

All the balloons travel in the same direction as they are BLOWN BY THE WIND.

A ground crew helps to hold the balloons down before they are READY FOR LIFT OFF.

It only takes around fifteen minutes to FILL THE BALLOON WITH AIR.

31

BIRD WATCHING *first* attracted a regular set of enthusiasts at the Park in the 1890s.

Many years ago, there were thousands of horses in New York. Now, there are far fewer, but you can still find them in Central Park offering CARRIAGE RIDES.

The MALLARD is the most common duck in the United States.

A red-tail hawk named PALE MALE became a permanent resident in 1992. The park rangers have named all of his mates, including his latest, dubbed Octavia, because she is his eighth.

Central Park is home to over 26,000 TREES and nearly 9,000 PARK BENCHES.

Central Park is often closed to traffic, making it popular with JOGGERS and ROLLER SKATERS.

While some of the park's areas are now "quiet zones," there are still plenty of spaces to hear BUSKERS, which have been a tradition of the park since it first opened.

MERLINS are small falcons with a powerful build. They patrol open areas looking for their prey.

New York's HULA HOOPING community often gets together for hoop jams in the park's open spaces.

NEW YORK, USA

32

HIT A HOME RUN IN
CENTRAL PARK

The DOWNY WOODPECKER eats food that larger woodpeckers cannot reach, such as insects living in the hollows of trees.

At the heart of New York City, USA, lies one of the world's most famous urban gardens, Central Park. Here there are several fields where games are played throughout the spring and summer, including baseball.

After the game, explore the rest of the park: photograph some of the 800 species that live here, take a paddle boat around the lake, visit the park's zoo, or stop for a hot dog or pretzel.

Watch out for resident RACCOONS with a taste for hot dogs!

The player who throws the ball at the batter is known as the PITCHER.

Central Park boasts 26 BALLFIELDS, as well as 30 tennis courts, 21 playgrounds, one carousel, and two ice-skating rinks!

RIVER-RAFT DOWN THE
GRAND CANYON

For more than six million years, the Colorado River has been carving out one of America's biggest icons: the Grand Canyon. Here, you'll feel like a tiny ant in the time of dinosaurs as you take a scenic float down the river surrounded by walls of ancient rock.

Strap in tightly as you and your guide paddle your way down the rapids. Then head ashore and set off on a hike. The Grand Canyon National Park is home to some of North America's most diverse wildlife: 355 bird species, 89 mammalian species, and 56 reptile and amphibian species.

MALE ELKS have large antlers made of bone, which are shed each year and grow afresh.

The Grand Canyon is home to one of the largest groups of PEREGRINE FALCONS in the world.

Research suggests that the GRAND CANYON took around three to six million years to form.

Only the female BLACK WIDOW SPIDER is poisonous, and she can be recognized by the bright red markings on her abdomen.

Watching from a distance is the best way to protect animals and helps keep wildlife WILD.

The tassel-eared squirrel, or ABERT'S SQUIRREL, is recognizable by its long ears with fluffy tufts.

The canyon is home to the GRAND CANYON RATTLESNAKE...

Check your boots before you put them on!

Around FIVE MILLION PEOPLE visit the Grand Canyon each year.

A BLACK RAVEN perches at the rim of the canyon, looking for its next meal.

The GOLDEN EAGLE can fly at speeds reaching 118 miles per hour.

A TURKEY VULTURE'S wingspan can reach 6.5 feet.

COUGARS, are the largest wild cat in North America.

There are nearly 40 DIFFERENT ROCK LAYERS that form the walls of the Grand Canyon.

COYOTES are excellent swimmers and will often escape predators by jumping into the river.

COLLARED LIZARDS have long sticky tongues to capture their prey.

Adult WILD TURKEYS have around 5,000 feathers.

A SCORPION'S TAIL contains a stinger with deadly venom glands.

Though they can't see very well, SCORPIONS have up to 10 eyes!

THE GRAND CANYON, USA

Steamboats were a popular form of transport before railroads were built. In the early nineteenth century, there were more than 1,200 cruising up and down the Mississippi.

The WETLANDS around the Mississippi river are rich with diverse wildlife.

DANCE ON THE DECK OF A
STEAMBOAT

Take a trip back in time on an original steamboat as you cruise down the Mississippi to the sound of jazz! The Mississippi is one of the world's great rivers, and many famous musicians such as Louis Armstrong and Bix Biederbecke have graced steamboat decks with soulful music as travelers soaked up the scenes of New Orleans.

Today, original steamboats have been restored to their former glory and traveling on one is like going to your favorite museum, where everything from the engine room to the deck is just as it was 200 years ago. Capture the Mississippi wilds on your camera as the jazz band liven up dinner time on the deck!

The MISSISSIPPI RIVER is about 2,317 miles long, and crosses 10 states in the USA.

THE MISSISSIPPI, USA

The GREAT EGRET has long legs for wading and a sharp bill for spearing fish in the water.

Dixieland music inspired a craze for LINDY HOP DANCING that swept North America in the 1920s and 30s.

DIXIELAND MUSIC is a style of jazz that originated in New Orleans.

Some of North America's largest CATFISH can be found in the Mississippi.

MARK TWAIN famously set many of his books on the Mississippi.

Louisiana is famous for its food, such as oysters, crayfish, and GUMBO, a Cajun stew.

There are around over 1.5 million AMERICAN ALLIGATORS in Louisiana State.

The paddle at the stern propels the boat forward and is POWERED BY STEAM.

37

The butterflies return to the SAME TREE each winter.

Monarch butterflies perform the LONGEST MIGRATION of any insect.

Monarch butterflies go through FOUR STAGES of development in their lifetime, from egg, to caterpillar, to chrysalis, to butterfly.

In the spring, the monarch butterflies return to their NORTHERLY BREEDING GROUNDS.

The male butterflies attract females by releasing chemicals from SCENT GLANDS on their hind wings.

Monarch butterflies are POISONOUS to predators such as lizards, birds, and mice—but are only harmful if you eat them!

Scientists aren't sure how the butterflies find their way to Mexico, but they think they NAVIGATE BY THE SUN.

38

MEET MILLIONS OF
MONARCH BUTTERFLIES

One of the world's most amazing natural events occurs every year in central Mexico, involving a particularly colorful creature: the monarch butterfly. As summer ends in North America, 35 million monarchs travel nearly 2,800 miles to their winter home in the boreal forests of Mexico's volcanic mountains.

Wake up early and join your small group of travelers on horseback deep into the forests where, as the sun rises, the monarchs fill the sky with their gold and orange wings.

Large areas of forest in Michoacan are protected in order to preserve the monarch butterflies' HABITAT.

Not all monarch butterflies migrate. Three generations are born and die within six weeks, but the FOURTH GENERATION lives for up to eight months...

The fourth generation's LONGER LIFESPAN allows it to migrate over the winter and return north to breed in spring, starting the cycle again.

MEXICO

Gulf of Mexico

Cuba

The Bahamas

Puerto Rico

St. Kitts and Nevis

Jamaica   Haiti   Dominican Republic

Antigua and Barbuda

Belize

Guatemala   Honduras

Caribbean Sea

Saint Vincent and the Grenadines

Dominica
Saint Lucia

El Salvador   Nicaragua   Panama

Barbados

Grenada

Costa Rica

Trinidad and Tobago

Explore ANCIENT TUNNELS in Castillo de San Felipe de Barajas (Colombia)

Count rainbows at ANGEL FALLS (Venezuela)

Colombia

Venezuela   Guyana   Surinam

Galápagos Isands

Ecuador

Explore the treetops of the AMAZON RAIN FOREST (Brazil)

Fish for PIRANHAS in Manaus (Brazil)

Meet a GIANT TORTOISE on the Galápagos Islands (Ecuador)

Stay in a JUNGLE LODGE in Cuyabeno National Park (Ecuador)

Brazil

Peru

Buy a BOWLER HAT (Bolivia)

See an ancient wonder of the world at MACHU PICCHU (Peru)

Bolivia

Pacific Ocean

See into space in the ATACAMA DESERT (Chile)

Paraguay

Pick the prettiest PARROT in Pantanal (Brazil)

Argentina

Uruguay

Chile

Spot the diving DOLPHINS in Ancud (Chile)

Ride with COWBOYS in Northern Patagonia (Argentina)

Dance the TANGO in Buenos Aires (Argentina)

Hear a GLACIER groan, Lago Argentino (Argentina)

Explore an AZURE CAVERN at Lake General Carrera (Chile)

CENTRAL & SOUTH AMERICA

Central and South America stretches from the equator down towards the icy Antarctic and packs a punch with its diverse and abundant wildlife, which can be found from its huge tropical rainforests to its freezing glaciers.

French Guiana

Cook up a feast with an ASADO (Brazil)

Throw some shapes in a CAPOEIRA CLASS in Salvador (Brazil)

Marvel at MODERNISM in Brasilia, (Brazil)

Dance the samba at the RIO CARNIVAL (Brazil)

Be a soccer fanatic in the MUSEU DO FUTEBOL in São Paulo (Brazil)

Atlantic Ocean

An art deco statue called CHRIST THE REDEEMER overlooks Rio from the Corcovado mountain. It is 100 feet tall and 90 feet wide.

Each samba school chooses a THEME for their costumes. This school have chosen the theme of birds.

The samba dance originated in the BAHIA REGION of Brazil around 1920.

About TWO MILLION PEOPLE are expected to take to the streets of Rio each day during Carnival.

BRAZIL

DANCE THE SAMBA AT THE
RIO CARNIVAL

Brazilians know how to throw a party better than anyone in the world! The most famous Brazilian festival, Carnival, is held just before Lent each year in many cities around Brazil, including Rio, and attracts more than two million visitors.

The best way to enjoy the festivities is to learn the steps to Brazil's traditional dance, the samba, and join one of the teams competing at the annual parade. Each of Brazil's samba schools have their own colorful costumes, and compete every night down the main streets of Rio. As you dance, you'll be joined by drummers and singers, twirling dancers, and performers on moving floats.

Schools are often led by a SINGER, who leads his or her performers in their unique school song.

At every Carnival, one woman will be named the QUEEN OF THE DRUMS.

The large bass drum used during the samba parade is called a SURDO.

The CAVAQUINHO is a small guitar similar to a ukulele, and is an essential instrument in samba parades.

The 200 samba schools are JUDGED on the originality of their elaborate floats, costumes, dancing, and musical performances.

43

The Amazon rainforest is under threat from DEFORESTATION.

It's thought that 2.5 MILLION SPECIES OF INSECT could live in the Amazon rainforest; 100,000 species have been discovered so far.

One of the most frequently seen animals in this rainforest is the COMMON SQUIRREL MONKEY.

The Amazon rainforest is made up of 390 BILLION TREES, with more than 16,000 different species to be found here.

The THREE-TOED SLOTH spends up to 20 hours asleep every day.

The TOUCAN uses its large colorful bill to pluck fruit from trees.

The AMAZON RAINFOREST is the largest one in the world.

The honey bear, or KINKAJOU, is not a monkey but more closely related to the raccoon.

LEAFCUTTER ANTS

EXPLORE THE TREETOPS OF THE
AMAZON RAINFOREST

SPIDER MONKEYS spend most of their lives in the treetops, eating and sleeping there.

Put on your rucksack and pick up your mosquito repellent—it's time to go on a jungle adventure! Most travelers have fantasized about a trip to the Amazon, which holds over half of the world's remaining rainforest, but not everyone has the opportunity to see it from the unique position of the treetops.

In recent years, giant walkways have been built between the canopies, and allow adventurers young and old to spot hundreds of exotic creatures—from above. Brazil is considered to have the greatest biodiversity of any country on the planet, with 55,000 plant species, 3,000 freshwater fish species, 689 different types of mammals, and 1,800 bird species. How many of these can you find here?

The RED-SPECTACLED AMAZON is a parrot named for the distinctive red markings on its head.

The HARPY EAGLE snatches its prey with powerful claws, which are as big as a bear's!

The CANOPY WALKWAY is suspended 115 feet in the air, giving you a fantastic view.

MACAWS are sociable birds that often form noisy flocks of up to 30 parrots.

LEAFCUTTER ANTS slice up vegetation by vibrating their powerful jaws a thousand times a second!

POISON DART FROGS

THE AMAZON

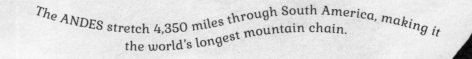

The ANDES stretch 4,350 miles through South America, making it the world's longest mountain chain.

GAUCHOS have lived a nomadic life herding cattle on the pampas for centuries.

The LASSO is a rope noose used for catching cattle.

The GREATER RHEA is a bird which cannot fly. Instead it runs using its long, powerful legs.

RIDE WITH COWBOYS IN
NORTHERN PATAGONIA

"Yee haw!" might be the only thing to shout as you set off to explore the foothills of the Andes Mountains in northern Patagonia— one of the best places to spend a day in the life of an authentic cowboy. Argentina contains lowlands called "pampas"—huge areas of farmland—which are often run by cowboys or "gauchos," as they are known in South America.

Take a ride through the rolling hills and along the gorges of the Andean water as the mighty Andes mountain range rises up behind you, or enjoy a more leisurely ride in a traditional horse and carriage. These are some of the best ways to explore this vast area and spot the creatures that inhabit it— which ones can you find here?

The PAMPAS were named after a native South American word, "pampa," which means "plain."

The ANDEAN CONDOR has a huge wingspan of up to 10.5 feet.

ARGENTINA

FLY FISHING is a popular sport practiced in the Andean lakes.

PAMPAS DEER

MAIZE, or corn, is often grown on the estancias, or ranches, on the pampas.

Every gaucho wears a PONCHO, a woollen blanket which can be worn, used as a saddle blanket by day, or as a blanket at night.

An ASADO BARBECUE is cooked by the gauchos. Argentina is famous for its delicious steaks.

The PAMPAS FOX tends to live on its own, hunting birds and rodents that live on the plains.

The BIG HAIRY ARMADILLO is covered in protective bony plates. It uses its powerful claws for digging.

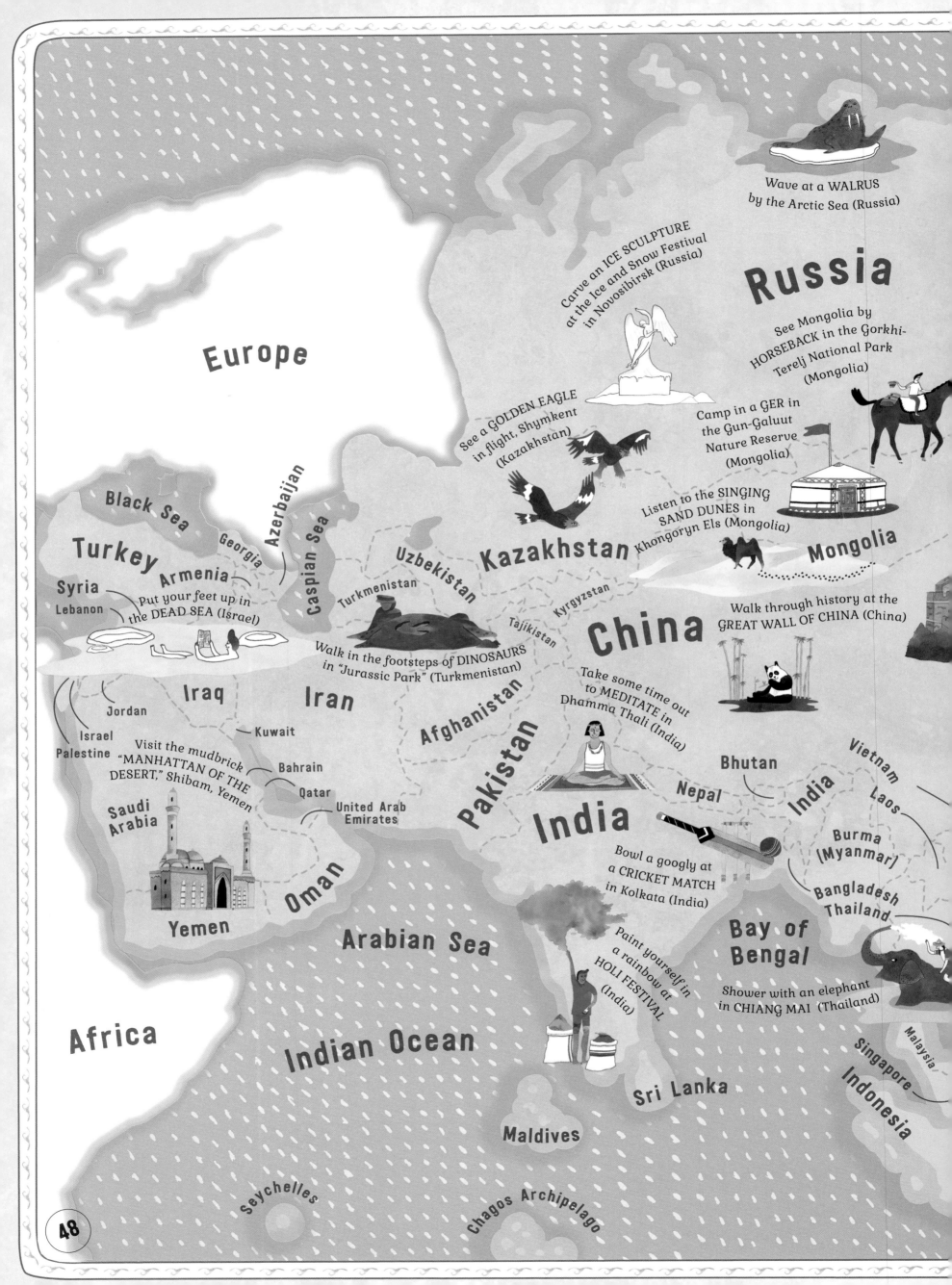

Wave at a WALRUS by the Arctic Sea (Russia)

Russia

Carve an ICE SCULPTURE at the Ice and Snow Festival at Novosibirsk (Russia) in

See Mongolia by HORSEBACK in the Gorkhi-Terelj National Park (Mongolia)

See a GOLDEN EAGLE in flight, Shymkent (Kazakhstan)

Camp in a GER in the Gun-Galuut Nature Reserve (Mongolia)

Listen to the SINGING SAND DUNES in Khongoryn Els (Mongolia)

Europe

Black Sea

Azerbaijan

Georgia

Caspian Sea

Kazakhstan

Mongolia

Turkey

Armenia

Uzbekistan

Kyrgyzstan

Walk through history at the GREAT WALL OF CHINA (China)

Syria

Turkmenistan

Tajikistan

China

Lebanon

Put your feet up in the DEAD SEA (Israel)

Walk in the footsteps of DINOSAURS in "Jurassic Park" (Turkmenistan)

Take some time out to MEDITATE in Dhamma Thali (India)

Iraq

Iran

Afghanistan

Jordan

Kuwait

Pakistan

Bhutan

Vietnam

Israel

Palestine

Visit the mudbrick "MANHATTAN OF THE DESERT," Shibam, Yemen

Bahrain

Nepal

India

Laos

Qatar

United Arab Emirates

India

Burma (Myanmar)

Saudi Arabia

Bowl a googly at a CRICKET MATCH in Kolkata (India)

Bangladesh

Yemen

Oman

Thailand

Arabian Sea

Paint yourself in a rainbow at HOLI FESTIVAL (India)

Bay of Bengal

Shower with an elephant in CHIANG MAI (Thailand)

Africa

Indian Ocean

Malaysia

Singapore

Sri Lanka

Indonesia

Maldives

Seychelles

Chagos Archipelago

Discover a LAVA LAKE at Kamchatka's Ring of Fire (Russia)

Take a trip back to the ICE AGE at the Mammoth Museum, Yakutsk (Russia)

See the sights from a FUNICULAR RAILWAY in Vladivostok (Russia)

Monkey around in Nagano's HOT SPRINGS (Japan)

ASIA & THE MIDDLE EAST

Asia is not only the world's biggest continent, it is the most populated, too. It is a land of contradictions: it offers adventures both ancient and modern and from the intrepid to the spiritual... Take your pick—you're sure to have fun!

North Korea

Japan

Be showered in CHERRY BLOSSOM (South Korea)

Bonin Islands

South Korea

East China Sea

Volcano Islands

Pacific Ocean

Put on a happy face at the FESTIVAL OF SMILES in Masskara (Philippines)

Set the world aglow at Hong Kong's LANTERN FESTIVAL (China)

Philippines

Cambodia

South China Sea

Find an undiscovered species in PAPUA'S FORESTS (Indonesia)

Brunei **Sabah**

Sarawak

Borneo

Celebes

Hang out with an ORANG-UTAN (Borneo)

Papua

Java **Sumba** **Flores** **East Timor**

Hot springs, or onsens, have been enjoyed by the Japanese for THOUSANDS OF YEARS, and are an important part of Japanese culture.

The water of the hot springs is RICH IN MINERALS and many people bathe in them to treat aches, pains and other medical conditions.

There are more than 3,000 ONSENS, or hot springs, across Japan. Traditionally, the bathers wear no clothing at all.

The Macaques enjoy the hot springs by day and retreat to the safety of the PINE FORESTS at night.

MACAQUES gather around the hot springs to bathe, play and meet possible mates.

MONKEY AROUND IN NAGANO'S
HOT SPRINGS

In the valley of the Yokoyu River lies the Jigokudani Monkey Park, a mountainous area known locally as "Hell's Valley" thanks to the steaming mists and bubbling waters that erupt out of the frozen ground. Because of the high altitude, the area is covered in thick snow for four months of the year, but, nevertheless, it is a popular destination for tourists who seek out the hot springs and pools of naturally hot water to bathe in.

The hot springs aren't only popular with human visitors; a large population of Japanese macaques can be found there year-round, escaping the cold by taking a dip in the hot water. Young adventurers may even be lucky enough to witness another thing we have in common with macaques: a snowball fight!

The macaque's DIET includes seeds, buds, leaves, bark, fruit and berries, as well as insects.

Macaques are one of only two known animals to WASH THEIR FOOD before eating it.

Macaques are the most NORTHERLY LIVING PRIMATE in the world (other than humans). They spend many months of the year in the snow.

The hot springs, or onsens, can be found in areas where there is VOLCANIC ACTIVITY.

Macaques can often be seen GROOMING one another as a way of bonding, helping each other to stay healthy.

Japanese macaques live in groups with a STRONG SOCIAL BOND, especially between females.

Young macaques have been observed entertaining themselves by MAKING SNOWBALLS.

JAPAN

The hot springs provide an essential SOURCE OF HEAT during the cold winter months—and what better way to warm up than take a hot bath?

The Lantern Festival coincides with the FIRST FULL MOON of the Chinese New Year.

The COLOR RED can be seen everywhere at this festival, because in Chinese culture it is thought to bring good fortune and joy.

The LANTERN FESTIVAL has ancient origins and has been celebrated for more than 2,000 years.

The Lantern Festival is a time when relations reunite and remember the IMPORTANCE OF FAMILY relationships.

Sweet rice balls called YUAN XIAO are traditionally eaten, to symbolize reunion and happiness.

SET THE WORLD AGLOW AT HONG KONG'S
LANTERN FESTIVAL

Chinese New Year is one of the only festivals celebrated all around the world—in any city where you can find a Chinatown, you are likely to find traditional Chinese street party celebrations. It is the most important holiday for the Chinese and during the two weeks in which it runs, Hong Kong is one of the most spectacular places to celebrate it.

On its first day, the streets of Hong Kong's Tsim Sha Tsui come alive with dancers, fire-breathing dragons and neon-lit floats. This is followed by an explosive fireworks display over Hong Kong's Victoria Harbor, which is known as one of the most impressive light displays anywhere in the world. The event to end the festival is also one that marks the beginning of spring: the Lantern Festival. On this day, lanterns are hung all over the city—in parks, restaurants and markets—and adventurers of all ages can join in by lighting one at night.

In ancient times the LANTERNS were made of red paper or silk, but today they can be found in all shapes, sizes and colors!

In the streets, the DRAGON DANCE is performed to scare away evil spirits and bad luck for the year ahead.

Many lanterns have RIDDLES on them to be solved by the children in the crowd.

HONG KONG

SHOWER WITH AN ELEPHANT IN
CHIANG MAI

Every day at around 9.45 a.m., a mix of laughter, splashing water and trumpeting can be heard in the forests of Chiang Mai: it's bath time for the elephants! This is a daily ritual at the Thai Elephant Conservation Center—a sanctuary and rescue center for distressed elephants from all over Thailand—and here, young adventurers can ride elephants into the shallows of the forest's river for their daily wash.

Elephants love water and bathe at least once a day—and sometimes twice in the hot season. There is no way to stay dry at this bath party: as the elephants wade in, they shoot jets of water into the air from their trunks and wallow on their sides as adventurers clean them of layers of mud. Others like to dump unsuspecting riders scrubbing the mud from their backs directly into the river!

ASIAN ELEPHANTS are slightly shorter and lighter than their African cousins, but the easiest way to tell them apart is by their much smaller ears.

Around five million people visit CHIANG MAI every year, drawn by its lush forests and wildlife.

Humans and elephants share a long history, and are depicted in friezes at Angkor Wat (in neighboring Cambodia) which date back to the TWELFTH CENTURY.

Historically, elephants were used in wars for transportation, and later in the logging industry. Today these practices are banned and elephants are employed mostly in TOURISM.

Elephants need a lot of care—and a LOT OF FEEDING! They consume 330 pounds of food and 40 gallons of water every day!

Elephants are becoming less common in the wild, largely due to the destruction of their NATURAL HABITAT.

There are around 5,000 ELEPHANTS in Thailand today—a much lower figure than 100 years ago, when there were more than 100,000.

An ELEPHANT'S TRUNK is fantastically strong and is able to lift heavy objects such as logs, but is dextrous enough to pick up an object as small as a coin.

The Thai Elephant Conservation Center has the prestigious job of caring for the ROYAL ELEPHANT STABLE of six male and four female white elephants.

A domestic elephant is usually gentle and careful around people and very loyal to its MAHOUT —the person that cares for it.

THAILAND

PAINT YOURSELF IN A RAINBOW AT
HOLI FESTIVAL

Spring is a time of new life all around the world—but nowhere is as colorful as India when it begins. The Holi Festival, also known as the "Festival of Colors" is celebrated across the country every year, and with music, dance and song it says goodbye to winter and welcomes spring with a rainbow of colors.

Adventurers young and old can take to the streets for an all out rainbow party! Sacks of colorful powder, flower petals and balloons filled with colored water are given to festival attendees, whose job is to throw them at as many people as possible! Once the great clouds of rainbow colors have subsided, young adventurers can enjoy the traditional foods like gujhiya while the singing continues well into the night.

Holi is celebrated the day after the first FULL MOON in the Hindu month of Phalguna (between February and March).

Holi is named for the Hindu demoness, HOLIKA, who was burned to death with the god Vishnu's help. A commemorative bonfire on the eve of Holi is one of the festival's highlights.

Don't expect special treatment if you are a visitor; anyone—FRIEND OR STRANGER— is considered fair game during Holi!

INDIA

Whilst Holi celebrates the arrival of spring and can be enjoyed by anyone, no matter their religion, it has its roots in HINDU LEGEND and mythology.

Water pistols and balloons are used in the free-for-all on the streets and DRIED PAINT is applied to people's faces.

Different areas of India have UNIQUE TRADITIONS during Holi...

in JAIPUR, an elephant festival is held...

and in UTTAR PRADESH, the women pretend to beat up men who try to steal sweets from them!

Women sing FOLK SONGS and perform TRADITIONAL DANCES during Holi, accompanied by men playing a drum called a dholak.

This festival is also seen as a time to FORGIVE AND FORGET past quarrels and rebuild relationships within the community.

SOCIAL BARRIERS and restrictions come down during Holi, creating a sense of togetherness between rich and poor, young and old.

BE SHOWERED IN
CHERRY BLOSSOM

There is one thing that signals the beginning of spring more than anything else in South Korea: the cherry blossom tree. For just a short time at the beginning of spring, cherry trees all over the country uncover their pink and white petals, and the place with the biggest concentration of these is the coastal area of Jinhae-gu.

Drawing more than two million visitors each year, young adventurers will be greeted by showers of flower petals as they walk along the Yeojwacheon boardwalk. Young and old can enjoy a pot of tea under the cherry canopy or the tastes of traditional Korean street food as the trees blossom and bloom all around!

Every spring, a TEN-DAY cherry blossom festival is held across the city which draws people onto its streets.

Traditional dress in Korea is known as HANBOK.

You're sure to enjoy a good brew here; TEA has long been an important aspect of Korean culture.

It's not just the blossoms that smell delicious; street food CAFÉS offer everything from "bibimbap" (rice and vegetables) to the more unusual "beondaegi" (boiled silkworm larvae).

A traditional sword dance known as "GEOMMU" has been performed in South Korea since the twelfth century.

58

ORNAMENTAL CHERRY TREES have been revered in East Asia for hundreds of years, and have been celebrated in the region's art, poetry and song.

Cherry trees are a member of the ROSE FAMILY, along with many other fruit trees.

There are over 1,000 kinds of cherry tree, but only a handful produce edible FRUITS.

Cherry trees need a COLD WINTER in order to thrive and produce their bewitching blossom the following spring.

The ONE MILE BOARDWALK is a favorite destination among couples looking for a romantic spot.

SOUTH KOREA

The Dead Sea is actually a SALT LAKE at the heart of the Middle East and is around 1,380 feet below sea level, which is Earth's lowest elevation on land.

The Dead Sea is situated between Jordan, Israel and Palestine in a DESERT, where there is very little rainfall.

The Dead Sea is fed by the River Jordan but it NEVER OVERFLOWS because the hot sun evaporates the water year-round.

The rocks are covered in SALT DEPOSITS, which are left when the saline water evaporates away.

Dead Sea mud is RICH IN MINERALS which are absorbed into the body when you rub it on.

The Ancient Egyptians would transport asphalt back from the Dead Sea to create balms used during the MUMMIFICATION PROCESS.

ISRAEL

PUT YOUR FEET UP IN THE
DEAD SEA

The Dead Sea may be the best place to read the newspaper and put your feet up—in water! At the lowest point on Earth, the Dead Sea is so full of salt that bathers just bob about on the surface: it is impossible to sink. This is because the quantity of water that evaporates from it is greater than that which flows into it, so even Olympic swimmers won't have an advantage here.

Young adventurers can spend the days floating the hours away, and later cover themselves in mud that collects in pools on the beach. Letting the mud dry in the sun before washing it off again in the sea is an essential experience in this part of the world: so don't be shy, and enjoy the mass mud bath!

Thanks to its low elevation, you are LESS LIKELY TO BE SUNBURNED in this area, as the air has high levels of bromine and other metals, which filter the sun's rays.

The water in the Dead Sea is almost TEN TIMES SALTIER than the world's other oceans.

The sea is so-named because its high levels of salt make it DIFFICULT FOR ANIMALS TO SURVIVE.

The Dead Sea was one of the world's first HEALTH RESORTS and is especially well-known for helping people with bad skin.

The water DOESN'T TASTE SALTY, but bitter instead, because it contains so many minerals.

Famous historical figures to have visited the Dead Sea include Herod the Great and CLEOPATRA!

AFRICA

Africa is home to nature's biggest and best-loved creatures... Trying to keep count here might prove tricky! But animals aren't the end of the story—look out and you'll discover a colorful tapestry of cultures and creativity.

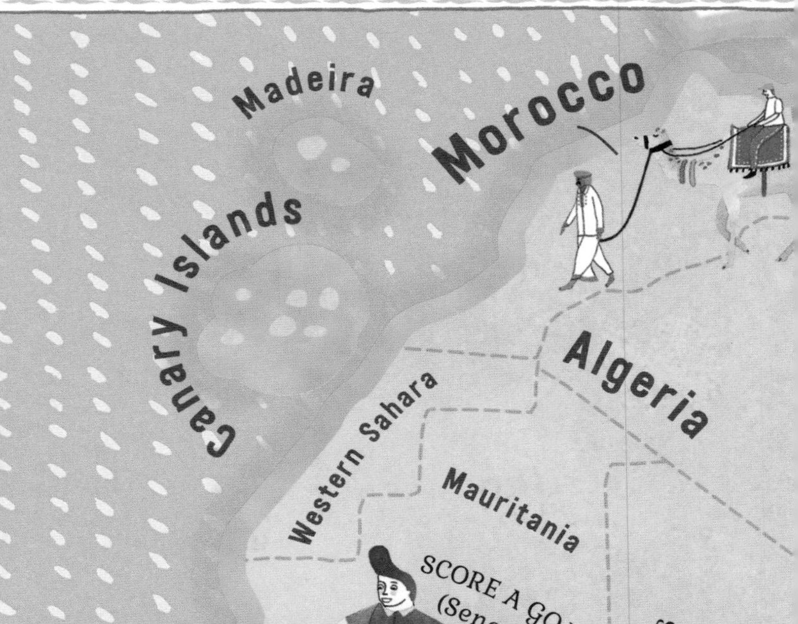

Madeira

Morocco

Canary Islands

Algeria

Western Sahara

Mauritania

Cape Verde

SCORE A GOAL
(Senegal)

North
Atlantic
Ocean

Senegal

The Gambia

Mali

DRESS TO IMPRESS
in Accra (Ghana)

Guinea-
Bissau

Guinea

Burkina
Faso

Sierra
Leone

Liberia

Ivory
Coast

Ghana

Togo

Ascension Island

St Helena

South
Atlantic
Ocean

Cross the Sahara in a
CAMEL CARAVAN (Morocco)

Tunisia

Libya

Explore Giza's ancient
PYRAMIDS (Egypt)

Egypt

Visit the oasis of
TIMIMOUN (Algeria)

Strike a deal in a SOUK (Egypt)

Benin

Niger

Chad

Sudan

Eritrea

The
Middle
East

Cook up a feast of
INJERA and WAT
(Ethiopia)

Djibouti

Nigeria

Play a part at the
AFRICAN THEATER FESTIVAL
for Children and Young People
in Yaoundé (Cameroon)

South
Sudan

Find a flock of
FLAMINGOS at
Lake Nakuru (Kenya)

Ethiopia

Somalia

Central
African
Republic

Cameroon

Equatorial Guinea

Gabon

See GORILLAS
in the mist
(Rwanda)

Congo

Democratic
Republic of
the Congo

Rwanda
Burundi

Uganda

Kenya

Watch the
MASAI WARRIORS
compete in the
jumping dance
(Kenya)

Sao Tome
and Principe

Angola

Go on a CANOE SAFARI down
the Zambezi River (Zambia)

Camp out in the
TARANGIRE TREETOPS
(Tanzania)

Tanzania

Malawi

Take a walk on
the WILD SIDE
(Mozambique)

Seychelles

Comoros

Mayotte

Indian
Ocean

Angola

Zambia

Zimbabwe

SANDBOARD down
a dune at Sossusvlei
(Namibia)

Botswana

Look out for
LIONS in the Kalahari
(Botswana)

Mozambique

Madagascar

Reunion
Mauritius

Namibia

Swaziland

Lesotho

Walk down an
avenue of BAOBABS
(Madagascar)

Swim with AFRICAN
PENGUINS at Boulders
Beach (South Africa)

South
Africa

Visit a
ZULU KRAAL
in Shakaland
(South Africa)

Mozambique Channel

The FACE OF THE SPHINX is thought to be modeled on Pharaoh Khafra, who was ruling at the time of its construction.

The sphinx is named after a Greek mythological beast, which had a woman's face, an eagle's wings and a lion's body. Its Arabic name translates as THE TERRIFYING ONE.

Pyramids were built as TOMBS for pharaohs and their families. The two smaller pyramids alongside Khufu are thought to have been built for his wives.

Egyptologists think that the sphinx once had a pharaonic BEARD and that the section of its missing NOSE was deliberately chiseled off by vandals.

It took roughly 20,000 PEOPLE to build the pyramids. These were once thought to have been slaves, but people now think that skilled craftsmen and paid laborers were used.

EGYPT

The sphinx is thought to have been built between 2558–2532 BC.

EXPLORE GIZA'S ANCIENT
PYRAMIDS

The simplest way to journey back in time a few thousand years is to take a trip to Egypt and spend a day at the pyramids of Giza. Here, you will find the "Great Pyramid": the oldest and largest of the three pyramids in the Giza Necropolis and the only remaining structure known as one of the Seven Wonders of the Ancient World.

Getting into the Great Pyramid of Khufu is an experience never to forget, but you may need to enter on your knees to get through the tiny doorways! Here young adventurers will find great chambers that housed the chambers of King Khufu made from just some of the estimated 2.3 million limestone blocks. Next, hop on a camel and visit the two smaller pyramids of Giza: Khafre and Menkaure. Finish your tour beneath the Great Sphinx, one of the most famous structures of the ancient world: a sculpture with a head of a man and the body of a lion!

Alongside the bodies, the Egyptians would bury things that they thought would be useful to their dead in the AFTERLIFE.

The Great Pyramid of Khufu is the oldest of the ANCIENT WONDERS OF THE WORLD.

It took approximately 2.3 MILLION BLOCKS OF STONE to build the Great Pyramid of Khufu, which has three burial chambers inside.

Rich men would pay to have their bodies preserved for the afterlife once they had died. This process was called MUMMIFICATION and took about 70 days.

ARTWORK has been found inside the tombs, which has helped us to understand how the Egyptians lived.

The unusual positioning of the pyramids has confused people for a long time. One theory is that they are placed directly beneath three of the stars in ORION'S BELT.

The Sahara is the WORLD'S HOTTEST DESERT and is 3.6 million square miles in size.

Many cave paintings show that the DRAA VALLEY was lush and fertile thousands of years ago, with many farming communities living there.

Less than FOUR INCHES OF RAIN falls in the Sahara Desert each year, making it difficult for animals and plants to survive.

Camel caravans have crossed these sands since the twelfth century, when SALT was discovered in the desert and transported out to be traded.

CROSS THE SAHARA IN A
CAMEL CARAVAN

There's only one desert that is the size of the USA, and that's the Sahara. Known for its perfectly sculpted, never-ending sand dunes, the Sahara crosses ten countries—Morocco, Mauritania, Mali, Algeria, Libya, Niger, Tunisia, Chad, Egypt and Sudan.

Most of the Sahara cannot be accessed by adventurers, but it is possible to travel across the Moroccan part of it on a camel caravan. Adventurers young and old can load their camels with supplies and then head off on a four day trek across the desert, hitching a camel ride when their legs become tired. Here, you'll discover that the desert isn't just sand: there will be plenty of rock art, villages to discover and fossils to find along the way.

Camels are hardy animals and can survive up to six months without food and more than a WEEK WITHOUT WATER.

In the mountains, you may come across a BERBER VILLAGE. Berbers are an ancient people who have lived in this region for more than 4,000 years.

CAMELS are well-prepared for the harsh conditions of the desert. They can shut their nostrils and have a third eyelid to keep out sand.

Camels store fat in their HUMPS, which they convert into energy when food and water is in short supply.

Although it is known for its hot, arid conditions, at night the temperature in the desert can plunge BELOW FREEZING.

Mankind has relied on camels for more than 3,000 YEARS for transportation, meat, fur, leather, and milk.

The Sahara desert is GROWING EVERY YEAR, partly because of overfarming and overgrazing of the land around its edges.

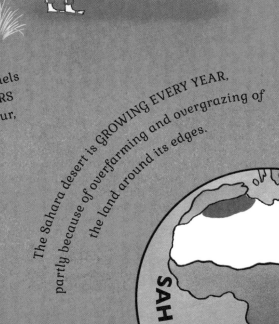

SAHARA DESERT

Whilst the cities of Senegal are modern and filled with high-rise buildings, out in the countryside, traditional MUD HUT VILLAGES can still be found.

SENEGALESE KAFTANS—pullover robes made of light fabric—are a stylish way to stay cool.

SCORE A GOAL IN

SENEGAL

Soccer may be the sport of choice for many nations, but there are few places where the people love it more than in Senegal. The national team of Senegal made its name when it defeated the reigning champions France in the first game of the World Cup in 2002, and since then you are likely to find games being played on every street corner that has a free patch of grass.

The atmosphere at national games often reaches fever pitch, and games in more informal settings can be just as lively! The cries of the spectators are often drowned out by the sound of horns, beating of drums and blares of the vuvuzela. Young adventurers should be prepared for some slinky footwork and expect a lot of celebration if they score the first goal!

SOCCER is the most played—and most watched—game in the world.

Soccer was introduced to Africa around 100 years ago by colonialists but was first invented over 3,000 years ago in ANCIENT CHINA.

SENEGAL

The national Senegalese soccer team have been nicknamed the LIONS OF TERANGA.

Soccer is a great way of keeping fit—players can run up to SIX MILES in a game!

Senegal is well known for its percussive music; often multiple DRUMMERS will play together to create complex rhythms.

Although the VUVUZELA is linked with soccer spectators in Africa, the plastic horn originally comes from Mexico.

69

GO ON A CANOE SAFARI DOWN THE
ZAMBEZI RIVER

If paddling down an open stretch of Africa's Zambezi River in a canoe doesn't sound like enough of an adventure—just look at the scenery! On the banks of the lower Zambezi you will see elephants, giraffes, lions and buffalo and many species of bird in their natural habitat, roaming freely as you float by.

The river flows through six countries—Angola, Namibia, Botswana, Zimbabwe, Mozambique and Zambia—and is home to hundreds of species of birds and animals, who depend on the river for water and food. Listen to stories and facts about the river as your guide steers you away from oncoming traffic... such as a hippopotamus! Adventurers of all ages agree that this is one of the best ways to see Africa's wildlife in all its untamed glory.

GIRAFFES are the tallest mammals on Earth. Look at their spots if you're wondering about their age: the darker the spots, the older they are.

PELICANS are easily identified by their large stretchy bills. They are unusual because they incubate their eggs with their feet.

ELEPHANTS are the world's largest land mammal. They use their large ears to radiate heat and keep cool on hot days.

If you see a HIPPOPOTAMUS, keep your distance! More people are killed by hippopotamuses every year in Africa than by any other animal.

HERONS are excellent fliers. Many are migratory, spending their summer in Europe and their winter in Africa.

If you're lucky, you might spot a LION in a tree, spending the day dozing, out of danger.

Lions are NOCTURNAL and head out in groups to hunt under the cover of darkness.

The BUFFALO is an herbivore and spends its days grazing. Its large horns help protect it from predators.

ZEBRAS have distinctive stripes, which help to confuse the eyes of any predators.

HIPPOPOTAMUSES keep cool in the African heat by wallowing in the water all day. They secrete a red substance from their skin which protects them from sunburn.

THE ZAMBEZI RIVER

AUSTRALASIA & OCEANIA

The world's smallest continent, Australia and Oceania, consists of around 25,000 islands, with climates which range from desert to tropical. With many uninhabited regions, expect an adventure wilder than anywhere else!

Join the MASK FESTIVAL (Papua New Guinea)

Papua New Guinea

Indonesia

Go snorkeling in the GREAT BARRIER REEF (Australia)

Hear a KOOKABURRA cackle in Cape York (Australia)

Go WALKABOUT in Kakadu National Park (Australia)

Walk the white sands of the WHITSUNDAYS (Australia)

CAMP out in the bush in Karlamilyi National Park (Australia)

See the sun set over ULURU (Australia)

Admire ABORIGINAL ART in Perth (Australia)

Australia

Cuddle a KOALA in Queensland (Australia)

Sail into SYDNEY HARBOR (Australia)

Care for a KANGAROO in Albany (Australia)

Wave at a WOMBAT in Adelaide (Australia)

Have a BARBIE ON THE BEACH on St Kilda Beach in Melbourne (Australia)

Indian Ocean

Tasmania

Flinders Island

Watch a PLATYPUS play (Tasmania)

Tasman Sea

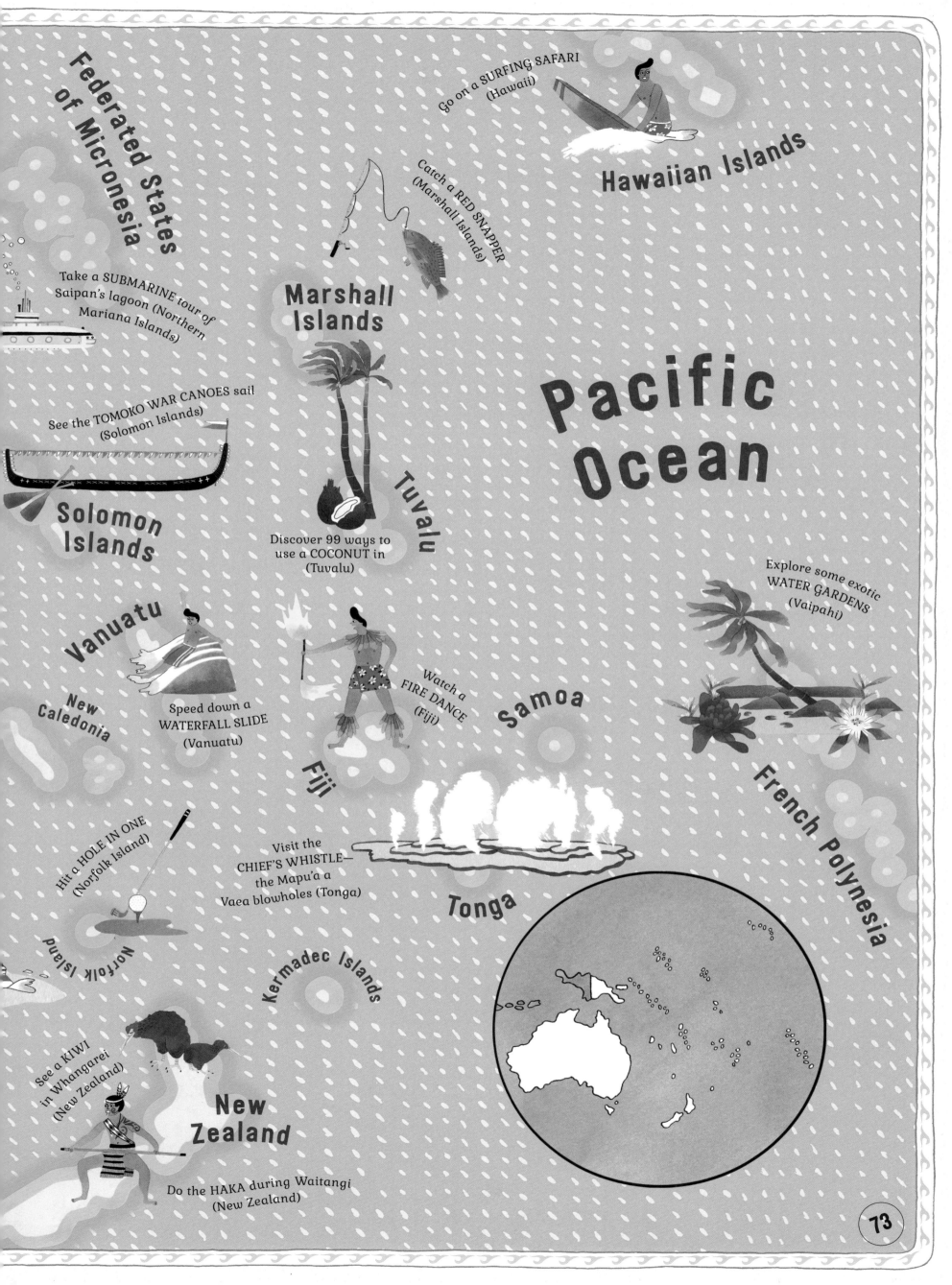

Go on a SURFING SAFARI
(Hawaii)

Hawaiian Islands

Catch a RED SNAPPER
(Marshall Islands)

**Marshall
Islands**

Take a SUBMARINE tour of
Saipan's lagoon (Northern
Mariana Islands)

**Pacific
Ocean**

See the TOMOKO WAR CANOES sail
(Solomon Islands)

**Solomon
Islands**

Tuvalu

Discover 99 ways to
use a COCONUT in
(Tuvalu)

Explore some exotic
WATER GARDENS
(Vaipahi)

Vanuatu

**New
Caledonia**

Speed down a
WATERFALL SLIDE
(Vanuatu)

Watch a
FIRE DANCE
(Fiji)

Samoa

French Polynesia

Fiji

Hit a HOLE IN ONE
(Norfolk Island)

Visit the
CHIEF'S WHISTLE—
the Mapu'a a
Vaea blowholes (Tonga)

Tonga

Norfolk Island

Kermadec Islands

See a KIWI
in Whangarei
(New Zealand)

**New
Zealand**

Do the HAKA during Waitangi
(New Zealand)

73

GO SNORKELING IN THE
GREAT BARRIER REEF

Diving the Great Barrier Reef might be the most colorful snorkeling experience in the world. Stretching over 1,240 miles along the eastern coast of Australia, this kaleidoscopic underwater world is one of the richest ecosystems on Earth.

Pull on your flippers and fasten your goggles before you lower yourself onto crystal clear water and swim your way over a floor of fish and coral treasures. How many different types of fish can you spot here?

The Great Barrier Reef is made up of at least 900 SEPARATE ISLANDS and 2,900 INDIVIDUAL REEFS.

PORPOISES are similar to dolphins but smaller and rounder in shape.

MASKED BUTTERFLYFISH can dart about the coral and hover on the spot thanks to their dorsal fins.

POTATO COD can grow up to 6.5 feet in length.

PINK ANEMONEFISH, also known as pink skunk clownfish, are able to change sex!

MAORI WRASSE are one of the largest coral reef fish.

SCUBA DIVERS

The GREEN TURTLE is the only herbivore of all the turtle species.

Once the GIANT CLAM fastens itself to a spot on the reef it stays there for life.

There are many other ways to see the reef: scuba diving, riding a SEMI-SUBMERSIBLE, or seeing it from above in a low-flying plane are popular alternatives.

The Great Barrier Reef is so big that it can be seen from OUTER SPACE.

GREEN ISLAND is a 6,000-year-old coral cay located in the Great Barrier Reef Marine Park.

CLOWN ANEMONEFISH live in anemones and are immune to their sting.

HAWKSBILL TURTLES are named for their beak-like snouts.

CORAL TROUT

A DUGONG, or "sea cow," has a flat tail and flippers like a whale but is more closely related to the elephant.

AUSTRALIA

This sculpture is a replica of a traditional Maori canoe, or WAKA, which was used for fishing and river travel, as well as warfare.

The Maori flag, the TINO RANGATIRATANGA FLAG, is raised alongside the New Zealand flag on Waitangi Day as a symbol of unity.

A HANGI is an "earth oven." Baskets of meat and vegetables are cooked in a pit on hot stones for several hours before they are devoured.

MAORI are the indigenous people of New Zealand. They migrated here over 1,000 years ago.

Traditional Maori clothing uses the fibres of native FLAX plants, which is woven into geometric patterns.

Food, known as KAI in Maori, is served in flax baskets called KONO. People eat sea eggs and REWENA, traditional Maori bread made with potatoes.

A HONGI is a traditional Maori greeting in New Zealand. It is done by pressing your nose and forehead to another person, who returns the gesture.

WAITANGI DAY commemorates the signing of a pact in 1840 between the British Empire and the Maori, which secured their rights as a people.

Traditional costumes of beaded waistbands called TATUA, straw skirts called PIUPIU, and feathered head ornaments are worn on Waitangi Day.

Traditional Maori arts are still practiced today in New Zealand, such as weaving, live dance, and performances and MOKO—tattooing.

WAR HAKAS were performed before a battle. It was thought to be bad luck if the performers weren't perfectly in time with each other.

DO THE HAKA DURING WAITANGI IN
NEW ZEALAND

"Ringa pakia! Uma Tiraha! Turi whatia!" These are the sounds of the traditional Maori dance, the haka, that you might hear on the beach at New Zealand's national holiday, Waitangi. Most people think the haka is a war dance—because the performers look so strong and fierce when doing it—but it is actually a dance that was simply made to show the fitness and power of each Maori tribe's warriors.

Today, many people recognize it from the pre-game performance of the All Blacks at rugby matches, as players wag their tongues and slap their chests to their native dance. Young adventurers might be lucky enough to learn one of the many hakas during the Waitangi holiday, when traditional Maori food, music, and customs celebrate New Zealand's rich indigenous culture.

GO ON A SURFING SAFARI IN
HAWAII, USA

Many countries are famous for having great surf beaches in the world, but the beaches of Maui are some of the best places to learn how to surf. Young adventurers will enjoy getting up, wobbling, falling off, diving under waves, and then trying it all again.

There are water sports for everyone in this area of the world: bodyboarding, windsurfing, and snorkeling, and plenty of golden sand to relax on afterwards. Some might be lucky enough to glimpse the sea turtles that come up to feed on the seaweed before dusk. Others might be looking out to sea at exactly the right time, when whales are known to traverse the area—can you see them on the horizon in this picture?

MAUI is one of the eight large, populated islands that make up the state of Hawaii. Hawaii became the fiftieth US State in 1959.

The warm waters of Maui are favored by HUMPBACK WHALES who breed, calve and nurse their young here.

GREEN TURTLES feed mostly on algae that grows on coral reeds and rocks close to shore.

There are two versions of surfing: SHORT BOARDING and LONG BOARDING.

The GREEN TURTLE is the most common turtle on the island of Maui.

Hawaii is the MOST ISOLATED place on Earth—it's 2,389 miles from its neighbor, California!

UNDERSEA VOLCANOES that erupted thousands of years ago formed the islands of Hawaii.

HAWAII, USA

WINDSURFING combines the art of surfing with sailing.

SURFING originated in Hawaii and is an important part of the state's culture.

All sorts of tropical fish, shrimp, crabs, and urchins live within the SHALLOWS of the Maui peninsula.

More than one-third of the world's commercial supply of PINEAPPLES comes from Hawaii.

Spot a SEI WHALE

South Orkney Islands

South Shetland Islands

Southern Ocean

Atlantic Ocean

Make a CAMP on the ice at Queen Maud Land

Spot a SOUTHERN RIGHT WHALE

Weddell Sea

Salute the EMPEROR PENGUINS at the Weddell Sea

Meet an ELEPHANT SEAL on Shetland Island

Alexander Island

Ronne Ice Shelf

Cross the ice on SNOW SHOES

Antarctica

KAYAK among the icebergs in the Bellingshausen Sea

Spot a SHAG

Ross Ice Shelf

Take a BOAT EXPEDITION across the Ross Sea

Go on a WHALE-WATCHING sea voyage in the Amundsen Sea

Ross Sea

Pacific Ocean

ANTARCTICA

Antarctica sits at the very bottom of our globe and is almost entirely covered in ice. Conditions here make it the coldest, driest, and windiest of all the continents, so be prepared for extremes when you set out on an adventure here.

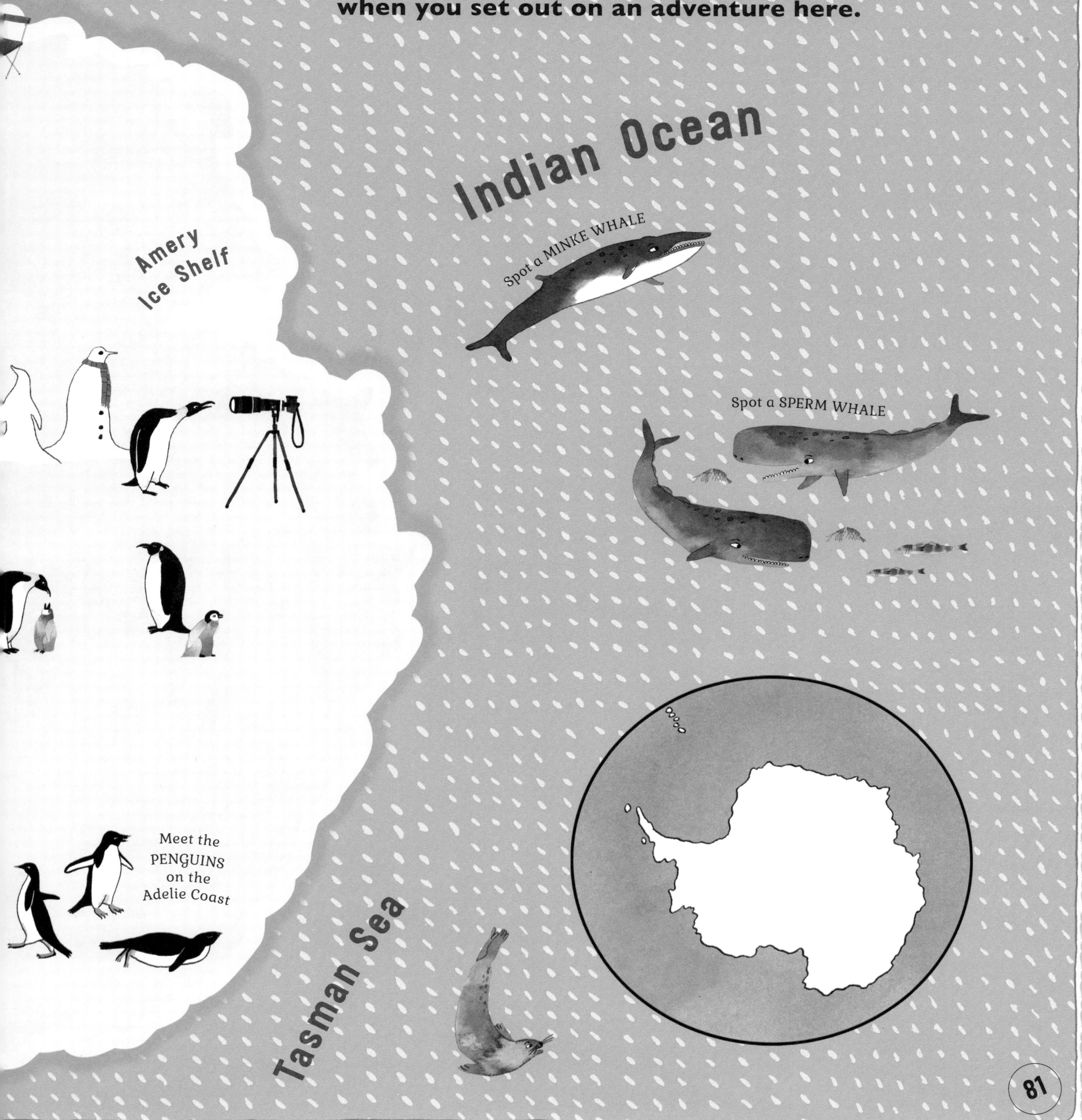

Indian Ocean

Spot a MINKE WHALE

Spot a SPERM WHALE

Amery Ice Shelf

Meet the PENGUINS on the Adelie Coast

Tasman Sea

VISIT THE PENGUINS IN THE
ANTARCTIC

The Antarctic is a land of extremes, with the coldest and driest conditions on Earth. Mostly untouched by humans, this land is an ultimate destination for any adventurer, and one of the only ways to get there is through the Antarctic Sound via boat and into the Weddell Sea.

Float by giant icebergs and travel through icicle tunnels as you make your way to Snow Hill Island and the best-loved creature of the region: the emperor penguin. These waddling wonders are the largest of all seventeen species of penguin, and the only species that inhabits the open ice of Antarctica during the winter. Adventurers are advised to visit during the summer, however, when the temperatures are less harsh and the whole array of Antarctic creatures come out to play!

The WEDDELL SEA is home to hundreds of fish and marine mammals. Scientists say its waters are cleaner than any other sea on earth.

The ANTARCTIC PETREL dives from the air into the icy waters to catch squid, krill, and fish.

Male penguins incubate their mate's EGG while the female goes out to feed.

EMPEROR PENGUINS huddle around their chicks to protect them from the icy winds of the Antarctic.

The ALBATROSS has the widest wingspan of any bird, and puts it to good use, traveling up to 620 miles a day.

ICEBERGS are created when a large chunk of ice breaks away from a glacier or ice sheet.

Ninety per cent of all the world's ICE and seventy per cent of the world's FRESH WATER is in Antarctica.

You can tell the age of ICE by its color. Old ice looks blue, because it has had any air bubbles squeezed out and is incredibly dense. Young ice, filled with bubbles, appears white.

THE ANTARCTIC

To keep WARM, penguins' bodies are insulated with a thick layer of blubber and covered in waterproof feathers.

The emperor penguin's tuxedo-like coat is a form of CAMOUFLAGE that helps keep them safe in water.

FEMALE EMPEROR PENGUINS hunt for meals of fish, squid, and krill.

HUMPBACK WHALES' flippers are a third of their total body length and are used for communication and feeding.

CAN YOU FIND?

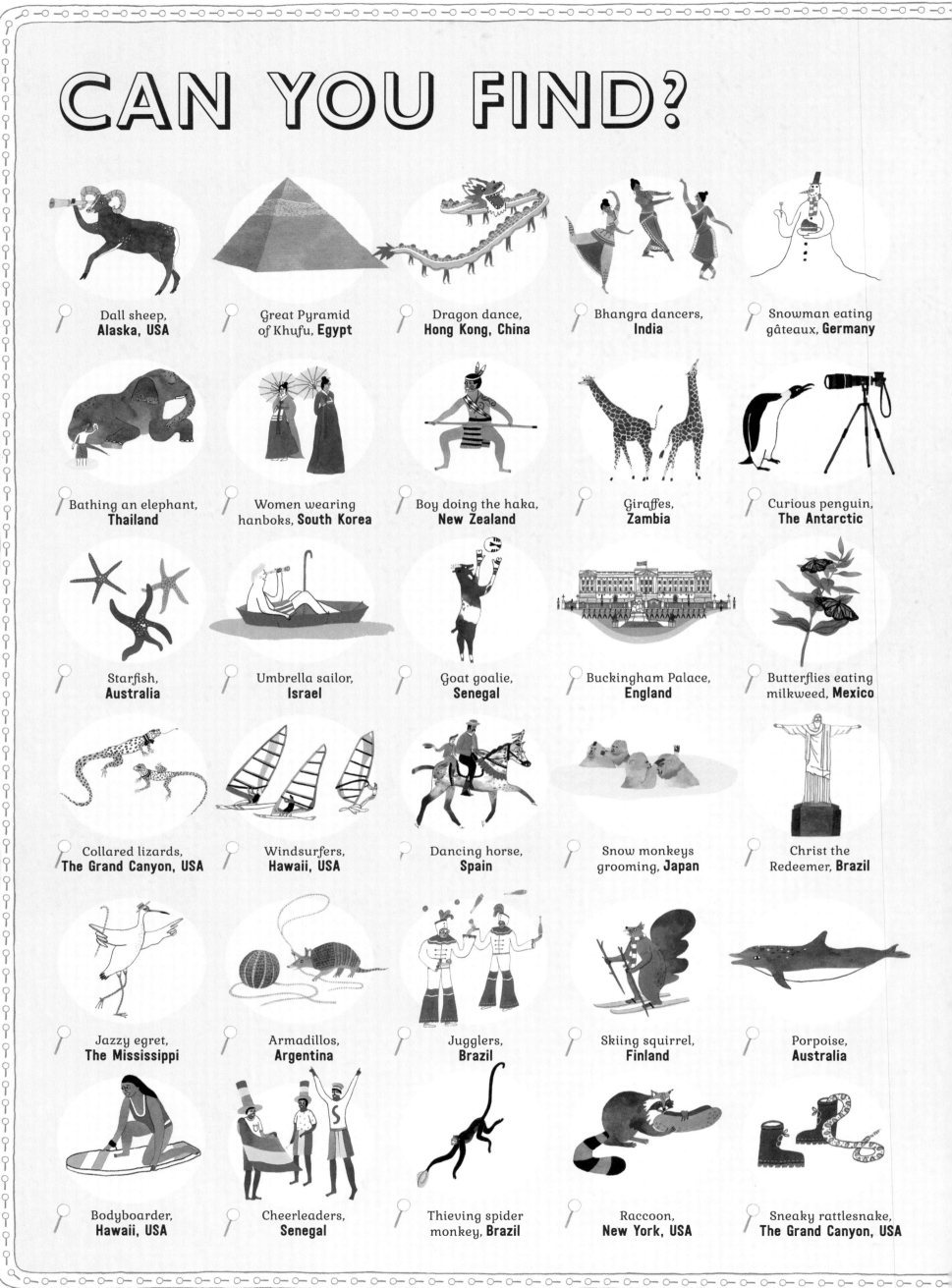

Dall sheep, **Alaska, USA**

Great Pyramid of Khufu, **Egypt**

Dragon dance, **Hong Kong, China**

Bhangra dancers, **India**

Snowman eating gâteaux, **Germany**

Bathing an elephant, **Thailand**

Women wearing hanboks, **South Korea**

Boy doing the haka, **New Zealand**

Giraffes, **Zambia**

Curious penguin, **The Antarctic**

Starfish, **Australia**

Umbrella sailor, **Israel**

Goat goalie, **Senegal**

Buckingham Palace, **England**

Butterflies eating milkweed, **Mexico**

Collared lizards, **The Grand Canyon, USA**

Windsurfers, **Hawaii, USA**

Dancing horse, **Spain**

Snow monkeys grooming, **Japan**

Christ the Redeemer, **Brazil**

Jazzy egret, **The Mississippi**

Armadillos, **Argentina**

Jugglers, **Brazil**

Skiing squirrel, **Finland**

Porpoise, **Australia**

Bodyboarder, **Hawaii, USA**

Cheerleaders, **Senegal**

Thieving spider monkey, **Brazil**

Raccoon, **New York, USA**

Sneaky rattlesnake, **The Grand Canyon, USA**

Cheeky camel, **Morocco**

Gondolier setting off, **Italy**

Giant clams, **Australia**

Ski jump, **Germany**

Black widow spider, **The Grand Canyon, USA**

Haggis hurling, **Scotland**

Hungry squirrel **Russia**

Coyote, **The Grand Canyon, USA**

Trinket sellers, **Egypt**

Waitangi boat sculpture, **New Zealand**

Lynx chasing hare, **Alaska, USA**

Throwing dried paint, **India**

Herd of reindeer, **Finland**

Funny hot air balloons, **Canada**

Buffalo and egrets, **Zambia**

School of damsel fish, **Australia**

Scottie dog, **Scotland**

Hanging New Year lanterns, **China**

Snowy owl, **Finland**

Drummers, **Brazil**

Juggling cowboy, **Argentina**

Acrobat penguins, **The Antarctic**

Hungry camel, **Morocco**

Sea turtles, **Hawaii, USA**

Croque monsieurs, **France**

Jazz band, **The Mississippi, USA**

Street food seller, **South Korea**

Bell tower of Santi Apostoli, **Italy**

N
W — E
S

INDEX